Title: Bargaining in real estate planning:Unlock the Power of Bargaining and Secure Your Dream Property.

I0436596

Pamela B. Palafoxl

Pamela B. Palafoxl

AUTHORS PAGE

Meet the magnificent mind behind the enlightening pages of "Bargaining in real estate planning"—Pamela B.Palafoxl emerges as a reference point for both old pros and excited lovers, with a significant understanding of the multifaceted dance of exchange and vital preparation in the powerful domain of land.

Drawing on extensive experience and a keen eye for market shifts, PamelaB.Palaoxl consistently

Pamela B. Palafoxl

weaves together functional bits of knowledge and hypothetical systems, creating an embroidery of shrewdness that influences anyone investigating the intricacies of land exchanges.

Their mastery transcends the ordinary, delving into the art of bartering with artfulness and key acuity.

Pamela's writing style is spellbinding, easily transforming complex ideas into accessible chunks of information.

"Whether you're a seasoned realtor looking to hone your skills or a newbie trying to grasp the complexities of the business, Pamela B.Palafoxl guides you with clarity and profundity.

Beyond the specifics, Pamela B.Palafoxl brings a passion for the subject that energizes the pages, making the investigation of land arranging a personal and vivid experience.

Every section demonstrates their commitment to providing readers with the tools they need to explore the ever-changing landscape of land debate.

Pamela B. Palafoxl

Past the details,Pamela B.Palafoxl brings a passion for the subject that animates the pages, making the investigation of land arranging a captivating and vivid experience.

Every section demonstrates their commitment to providing readers with the tools they need to explore the ever-changing landscape of land exchange.

Pamela B.Palafoxl doesn't simply bestow information in "Bargaining in real estate planning ,"

They light an anomaly that pushes readers to think fundamentally, haggle in a calculated way, and succeed in the difficult universe of land.

This book stands as a testament to Pamela B.Plafoxl's dedication to ushering in a new era of realtors equipped with insight and foresight.

Pamela B. Palafoxl

What is bargaining? Bargaining is a simple form
of the distributive negotiation process that is
both competitive and positional

Pamela B. Palafoxl

,INTRODUCTION

PRESENTATION

Welcome to a world where sharing becomes a kind of fine art and every relationship has the capacity to transform.

This book, "Bargaining with Results," will take you on an intriguing journey that delves into the subtleties of trade and reveals the secret to achieving unexpected outcomes.

Pamela B. Palafoxl

The ability to bargain has truly become a crucial skill in a constantly changing environment full of conflicting interests and points of view.

The capacity for handling artfulness can have a big impact on agreements, personal relationships, or everyday experiences.

Either way, this book is more than just another exchange strategy tool.

It deviates from protocol and takes you on an introspective exploration of
Whether you're a carefully prepared moderator trying to refine your abilities or a fledgling moving into the universe of dealing, "Bargaining with Results" is your crucial aid.

A book rises above ventures and callings, offering widespread rules that can be applied to any discussion situation.

All in all, would you say you are prepared to change the manner in which you arrange? Is it true that you are ready to revise the guidelines and open a universe of potential outcomes?

Pamela B. Palafoxl

Provided that this is true, then, at that point, go along with us on this elating excursion as we dive into the specialty of dealing with results.

From the meeting room to the lounge, this book will engage you to haggle with certainty, accomplish noteworthy results, and make enduring effects.

Prepare to leave with an exceptional experience.

Your journey to becoming an expert moderator starts now.

Pamela B. Palafoxl

Pamela B. Palafoxl

CHAPTER 1

An introduction to negotiation

We negotiate a great deal – more than we realize.
Sometimes it goes smoothly, sometimes it seems difficult. While there is much advice about how to negotiate and be a 'winning negotiator', the actual experience does
not seem as straightforward as books suggest.

Why? Because negotiation is a complex process.

This book grapples with these complexities while recognising the idiosyncrasies of both the negotiation process and the
negotiator.

Pamela B. Palafoxl

This opening chapter explores some core complexities of negotiation, providing a foundation for later chapters.

Although this book will focus on the business context, the principles and skills can be applied in other contexts such as interpersonal negotiation, sales or when resolving legal, environmental and social issues.

Very few people are employed solely as professional negotiators; for most of us it is just an integral,perhaps unrecognized, part of our job.

This book also shows that throughout an organization, negotiation is deeply embedded as a way of getting things done.

The advice offered in this book is based on good research yet is pragmatic,recognising the difficult contexts within which negotiations take place.

Pamela B. Palafoxl

Recommendations that seem to be at the heart of the many suggestions that emerge throughout the ensuing chapters.

These are not five keys to success but are offered,along with the rest of the book, with the aim of guiding the reader's progress towards being a better negotiator.

Pamela B. Palafoxl

CHAPTER 2

A-Z Bargaining Terms

1•A

 **agotiation Agenda A** formal agreed upon list of goals to be achieved or items to be discussed in a particular order during a meeting or negotiation.

Agendas can be formal and obvious, or informal and subtle in negotiations.

Pamela B. Palafoxl

A negotiation agenda can be used to control the negotiation meeting.

B•Negotiation Agent

A person who acts for or in place of another individual or entity as their representative in a negotiation with a third party.

An agent, sometimes referred to as a third party agent, has full or limited authority to act on the behalf of the party they represent.

C•Negotiation Anchoring
Anchoring is an attempt to establish a reference point (anchor) around which a negotiation will revolve.

The anchor will often be used as a reference point to make negotiation adjustments.

Anchoring often occurs when the first offer is presented at the beginning of a negotiation.

D•Arbitration

Pamela B. Palafoxl

A process to resolve a dispute between negotiating parties who have reached a deadlock in their negotiation.

The parties in dispute are referred to a 'third party', which is one that is either agreed upon by the parties in dispute, or as provided by legisled law.

The third party renders a [judgment] that is binding on the parties in dispute.

Arbitration is often used in international negotiations and in collective bargaining.

E•Aspiration Base

Setting the highest achievable negotiation target level in terms of goals or objectives to conclude a negotiated agreement.

2•B
Negotiation Bargaining

What is bargaining? Bargaining is a simple form of the distributive negotiation process that is both competitive and positional.

Meaning bargaining doesn't seek to create value but instead focuses on negotiators claiming value.

Bargaining very often revolves around a single issue—usually price.

B•Negotiation Bargaining Zone

Your Bargaining Zone is the range or area in which an agreement is satisfactory to both negotiating parties.

The bargaining zone is essentially the overlap area between walk away positions in a negotiation.

C•BATNA

BATNA is an acronym popularized by Roger Fisher and William Ury which stands for 'Best Alternative to a Negotiated Agreement'.

BATNA answers the question: 'What would you do if you weren't able to agree a deal with your negotiation counterparty?' Your

BATNA is the alternative action you'll take should your proposed agreement fail to materialize. Most business people simply use the phrase: 'Best Alternative'.

3•C
Negotiation Coalition
temporary union between two or more individuals or groups for a common aim or goal.

A relatively common practice utilized in multi-party negotiations, used to gain advantage in the negotiation.

Coalitions are more common when negotiators' stand to gain more through collaboration than through competing.

A•Collective Bargaining
A negotiation process that occurs between employers (or their representatives) and the representatives of a union to negotiate issues that

consist of wages, hours of work and other conditions of employment.

Normally results in a written contract that is defined by specific time duration – 'life of the contract'.

Pamela B. Palafoxl

Doesn't necessarily consist of bargaining as the name suggests.

Learn more about Collective Bargaining

B•Common Ground
This term refers to the area of agreement or a basis for an understanding that is mutually agreed upon by all parties to a negotiation.

C•Concession Strategy
Your concession strategy is a plan of the goals / positions and sometimes the underlying interests that you will be trading with the other party.

Before you enter the negotiations, at the very least you should have clarity on your and the other party's goals, and a sequence of which goals you want to trade or exchange.

Concession strategies vary in detail. 'Concession Strategy' is more accurately called the 'Trading Plan'.

D•Negotiation Concessions
Negotiation Concessions are also sometimes referred to as 'trade-offs' where one or more

parties to a negotiation engage in conceding, yielding, or compromising on

issues under negotiation and do so either willingly or unwillingly.

Negotiation Concessions often include 'log rolling'.

E•Negotiation Constituent

A constituent is someone or a group on the same side of the negotiating party but who exerts an independent influence on the outcome through the principal negotiator, or

to whom the principal negotiator is accountable.

For example, a union negotiator must have an agreement voted upon by the union members (constituents) before it can be ratified as an agreement.

F•Counter Purchase
An arrangement where one company (the seller), agrees to sell products or services to

a foreign purchaser, but also simultaneously agrees to purchase specified products or services from the foreign partner.

Also known as parallel bartering and is the most commonly used form in a countertrade agreement in international business interactions.

G•Countertrade Agreement
An international trade arrangement with a foreign business partner.

A barter system whereby the parties agree to exchange, or purchase (buy back) for

resale, goods or services in exchange for another type of goods or services.

Goods or services exchanged may be used in the primary product or service being sold.

H•Negotiation Counterparty

In a negotiation, a counterparty (counterparties – plural) is the other representative(s) of the other

negotiation party(s) with whom one is negotiating a potential agreement or contract.

Pamela B. Palafoxl

4•D
Debt Negotiation

A negotiation process where the debtor negotiates the amount, timing and any other

terms of a loan such as arrears, liability, or balance owed to the creditor(s).

A•Distributive Negotiation

A distributive negotiation type or process that normally entails a single issue to be negotiated.

The single issue often involves price and frequently relates to the bargaining process.

Also referred to as 'Win – Lose', or 'Fixed – Pie' negotiation because one party generally gains at the expense of another party. 'Win - Win'

negotiation is conversely often referred to as Integrative Negotiation.

5•F
Negotiation Facilitator

This is usually a mutually agreed upon neutral third party to lead a complex meeting of two or more parties involved in a

negotiation. Often employed in 'multi party' negotiations.

Their purpose is to organize, aid, and offer assistance in helping the negotiating parties

find their own solutions on the issues under discussion.

B•Negotiation Framing

A means to process and [organize] information.

A frame provides a perspective of the problems or issues for a decision maker.

One can use a frame to understand the importance of facts or issues in relation to each other.

One can use this understanding of the facts or issues to then determine possible outcomes and consider contingency actions to solve a problem.

Pamela B. Palafoxl

Using a framework can allow you to consider all potential gains and losses and available options for any situation.

6•G
Negotiation Game

A few negotiation training courses make use of negotiation simulation exercises delivered using online negotiation training games.

In this way, technology can be leveraged to teach participants essential principles of negotiation, psychology or influence in a fun and interactive environment.

Some games are played between pairs, whilst others involve a room full of people.

The purpose of most negotiation training games is to win, and sometimes to avoid losing.

Many negotiation games leave the decision of what 'winning' or 'losing' means to the players.

Negotiation role-play exercises prevalent in most courses should not be confused with negotiation games.

Pamela B. Palafoxl

7•H
Negotiation Haggling

Haggling means to negotiate, argue, bargain or barter about the terms of a business transaction, usually focussing on the purchase or selling price of a product or service,it's a form of distributive negotiation.

A•Hostage Negotiation

A negotiation conducted between law enforcement agencies, diplomatic or other government representatives for the release of a person(s) held hostage against their will by criminal, terrorist or other elements.

8•I
Initial Public Offering (IPO)

A company's first sale of stock to the public.
The IPO is usually tendered, but not always, by those of young, smaller companies attempting to

locate equity capital and a public market for their stock.

An IPO may present considerable risk but also has the potential of significant profits for investors. Investment companies (closed end funds) generally include underwriting fees which represent a load which is then passed onto buyers.

A•Integrative Framework

A means of negotiation decision making to [conceptualize] the actions, contingencies of all possible outcomes, options and scenarios.

Applied to integrative negotiations with the intention of incorporating the goals and aims of all the negotiating parties to create

maximum value through collaborative negotiation.

B•Integrative Negotiation

Integrative negotiation is often referred to as "win-win" and typically entails two or more issues to be negotiated.

It often involves an agreement process that better integrates the aims and goals of all the involved negotiation participants through creative and collaborative problem-solving.

Relationships are usually more important, with more complex issues being negotiated than with distributive negotiation.

C•Interests in Negotiation

Negotiation interests are considered to be the motivating factor(s) and the underlying reasons behind the 'negotiation position' adopted by a negotiation party.

Negotiation interests often entail some combination of economic, security,

recognition, and control issues, or the desires, concerns, aims or goals of a negotiating party in a negotiation process.

D•Internal Negotiation
A process that occurs between two or more members or colleagues of the same company, organization or constituency.

Pamela B. Palafoxl

Colleagues need to negotiation internally usually with their stakeholders - most especially when preparing for an external

client, supplier, government, regulatory body or other negotiation.

The word 'preparation' is often used interchangeably with the phrase 'internal negotiation'.

The differing reward structures, motivations and psychology play a major role in

ensuring that internal negotiations are often as challenging as external negotiations.

The most popular way to prepare with your colleagues or stakeholders is via a physical meeting or a conference call.

9•J

Joint Venture Agreement

A contractual agreement between two or more business partners to assume a common business strategy on a project.

All partners generally agree to share the profits and losses through their common shareholdings.

Pamela B. Palafoxl

10•L
Litigation

A formalized legal process to resolve a dispute through legal action in the form of a lawsuit.

It often entails a contractual issue. It is the act of either bringing or challenging a lawsuit.

A•Negotiation Logrolling

A negotiation exchange that involves making negotiation concessions or the 'trading-off' of issues so as to [maximize] on each sides' value.

So you will offer the other side something that they value more than you, in exchange

for gaining something from them that you value more than they do. (Also: Log Rolling)

B•Lose-Lose Negotiation
A negotiation result where all parties to a negotiation leave resources or gold on the table at the conclusion of a negotiation and fail to

recognize or exploit more creative options that would lead to a 'win-win' negotiated outcome.

A term also used in 'Game Theory' and Economics.

C•Lose-Win Negotiation

Lose-Win refers to a distributive negotiation where one negotiator's loss is the other negotiator's gain.

Both negotiators are typically competing to claim the most value from a 'fixed pie' or value negotiation.

The term 'lose-win' was popularized by 'Game Theory'. This is a form of a zero-sum game. (The inverse is known as Win - Lose Negotiation).

11•M
Majority Rule

A concept often employed in 'Group' or 'Multi Party' negotiations to achieve consensus or agreement.

Pamela B. Palafoxl

As the term implies, a decision or agreement is reached after having been voted upon and decided in [favor] by a majority of the parties present at the negotiating table

A•Mediation

Mediation usually consists of a negotiation process that employs a 'mutually agreed' upon third party to settle a dispute between

negotiating parties to find a compatible agreement to resolve disputes.

B•Negotiation Meeting

Negotiation meetings are typically where most of the deal is negotiated, with business

negotiation meetings these days being face to face and via voice.

The proper planning and effective running of negotiating meetings can make or break a deal.

The more complexity involved, the more important getting the negotiation meeting planned correctly becomes.

C•Merger and Acquisition Negotiation

Pamela B. Palafoxl

A negotiation process conducted for the merger or joining of two companies into a single business entity, or the outright
purchase of a company by another company.

D•Multi Party Negotiation

A negotiation that involves more than two negotiating parties in a negotiation.

D•Multiple Offers

A technique sometimes employed to offset the possibility of anchoring in an integrative negotiation.

Multiple offers are two or more offers or proposals of relatively equal value that are presented simultaneously to invite greater discussion of the issues under negotiation.

12•N
Negotiation
Negotiation is an interactive process between two or more negotiators or parties

seeking to find common ground on issues of mutual interest, where the negotiators or parties seek to make a mutually acceptable agreement that will be honored by all.

13•P
Negotiation Position

Negotiators' positions are the things they demand you give them and also the things that they refuse to provide you with.

Negotiation positions are typically communicated in meetings, emails, and proposals.

Inexperienced negotiators too often take the positions of the other side at face value and

don't probe with questions or challenge sufficiently.

A•Negotiation Principal
The primary decision making authority in a negotiation.

Pamela B. Palafoxl

Third party agents will often represent the interests or objectives of a principal in a negotiation.

B•Principled Negotiation
Principled negotiation is an interest-based approach to negotiation that focuses primarily on conflict management and conflict resolution.

Principled negotiation uses an integrative approach to finding a mutually shared outcome.

C•Negotiation Procurement Solution

Business services provided by internal specialists or external vendors or consultants.

Procurement Solutions includes skills development ranging from purchasing or procurement training, coaching, consulting or other education services, as well as input on any procurement procedure as it relates to any aspect of the supply chain.

Three main areas include sourcing costs, logistics management and aspects of manufacturing.

Typical focal areas include achieving price reductions, technology, reverse auctions, information systems, transport and shipping, working capital (e.g. inventory and payment terms), and automation.

D•Purchase Order Financing

The assignment of purchase orders by a business to a third party who accepts responsibility for billing and collecting from buyers of the company's products and services.

It is a form of expensive financing used to purchase materials required to produce products needed to [fulfill] a purchase order already received from a buyer.

14•R
Negotiation Rapport

Pamela B. Palafoxl

Rapport happens across a number of levels. In business, most people associate rapport with matching and mirroring body language.

Rapport brings you and the other party you're seeking to influence into sync. When done well, rapport is undetectable, and works at the unconscious level.

Rapport is more difficult to detect on the auditory level.

So if you adjust your volume, cadence, inflection, pitch, resonance, length of sentences to that of the person or people you're seeking to influence, you'll be more

likely to be listened to and enjoy more understanding and agreements.

Rapport can also occur at the level of beliefs and values.

When you discuss similarities in your beliefs and values, you're more likely to enjoy a deeper sense of rapport.

Storytelling is powerful for this reason.

Pamela B. Palafoxl

A•Negotiation Reciprocation

The act of making a similar or like exchange of something in return for something given by one party to another party.

In a negotiation, this could entail an exchange of information and/or an

exchange of concessions between the negotiating parties.

B•Reservation Price

The reservation price is the least favorable point at which you will accept a negotiated agreement.

For example, for a seller this means the least amount (minimum) or bottom line they would be prepared to accept.

For a buyer, it would mean the most (maximum) or bottom line that they would be prepared to pay.

Pamela B. Palafoxl

It is also sometimes referred to as the "walk-away" point.

C•Risk-Averse

A low level or approach in the amount of risk that a negotiator is prepared to accept in a negotiation.

A negotiator who decides to accept the "sure thing" where a result is certain to be achieved is said to be "risk-averse", and is

not willing to gamble further on a potential negotiated result.

D•Risk-Seeking

A high level or approach in the amount of risk that a negotiator is prepared to accept in a negotiation.

A negotiator who decides to gamble rather than accept the 'sure thing', and who has the

Pamela B. Palafoxl

expectation that they will gain more in a negotiation is said to be 'risk-seeking'.

15•S
Salary Negotiation

Salary negotiation is a process where one party (usually the employee) negotiates the amount of their pay, income, earnings, commission, salary, wages, wage remuneration, annual review, or salary raise with another party (usually a representative of the employer, such as their manager).

A•Negotiation Skills

What are negotiation skills? Negotiation skills are required to secure better agreements in our personal and business lives.

Negotiating skills include methods of:

B•Negotiation Strategy

A predetermined approach or prepared plan of action to achieve a goal or objective to make an

Pamela B. Palafoxl

agreement or contract. (also see Negotiation Tactics.)

C•Negotiation Styles
The most popular way to divide the typical negotiation styles or approaches are:

16•T
Negotiation Tactics

Negotiation tactics are the detailed methods employed by negotiators to gain an advantage.

Negotiation tactics are often deceptive and manipulative.

Often, negotiators use negotiation tactics to fulfill their own goals and objectives.

This is often to the detriment of others, making most tactics in use today "win-lose" by nature.

A•Negotiation Target

Pamela B. Palafoxl

The desired negotiation outcome or goal is decided at the start of the negotiation.

This is best set across each and every aspect of a negotiation (e.g. price, term, volume etc).

Some organizations set an ambitious negotiation aspiration or opening offer, and a less ambitious negotiation target, while for others these are one in the same.

The level of negotiation aspiration is heavily influenced by a country's culture, with the

Germans setting lower aspirations and the Chinese higher.

A•Negotiation Trade-Off

Also sometimes referred to as a 'Concession' where one or more parties to a negotiation engage in conceding, yielding, or compromising on issues under negotiation and do so either willingly or unwillingly.

Pamela B. Palafoxl

B•Negotiation Trading Plan

A negotiation trading plan is a table or spreadsheet that sets out which goals /

positions / tradables you are going to exchange or trade with the other party.

CHAPTER 3

Types of Negotiation

F urthermore, Negotiation also fosters creativity and innovation.
Parties can collaboratively brainstorm and solve problems.

They can explore alternative options and develop innovative solutions that may have otherwise been overlooked.

The process encourages out-of-the-box thinking and encourages parties to consider multiple perspectives.

This leads to better outcomes and win-win situations.

Moreover, the two facets of Negotiation:

•conflict resolution and

•effective communication, contribute to effective Negotiation.

These facets have broader applications in everyday life, enhancing personal relationships, teamwork, and collaboration.

A look at the Types of Negotiation

A comprehensive understanding of the various Negotiation Types can empower individuals to adapt their strategies and tactics to specific contexts.

Here are the five common Types of Negotiation described in detail:

Types of Negotiation

1) Distributive Negotiation

Distributive Negotiation, also known as Positional or Competitive Negotiation, is a win-lose approach.

This is where the parties involved in the Negotiation perceive the situation as a limited resource.

They aim to claim the largest possible share for themselves.

Each party tries to maximize their gains while minimizing their concessions.

Parties can collaboratively brainstorm and solve problems

Additionally, Distributive Negotiation often involves fixed or zero-sum issues.

Pamela B. Palafoxl

Here, one party's gain is directly correlated with the other party's loss.

Skilled negotiators focus on Assertiveness, strategic positioning, and effective bargaining to secure favorable outcomes.

2) Integrative Negotiation

Integrative Negotiation, also referred to as Interest-based or Collaborative Negotiation, is a win-win approach.

Parties seek mutually beneficial solutions by identifying shared interests and exploring creative options.

Unlike Distributive Negotiation, this type expands the radar, aiming for outcomes that satisfy the needs and interests of all parties involved.

This approach emphasizes collaboration, problem-solving, and effective communication.

Skilled negotiators in Integrative Negotiation focus on active listening and empathy.

They also aim to generate value to create sustainable and positive outcomes.

3) Competitive Negotiation
This is one of the powerful Types of Negotiation, also known as Hard or Tough Negotiation.

It involves assertiveness and aggressive tactics.

In this approach, negotiators prioritize their own interests and goals, often at the expense of the other party.

Additionally, competitive negotiators may use tactics such as bluffing, threats, or excessive demands to gain an advantage.

The competitive style can be effective in certain situations, but it can also strain relationships and damage long-term prospects.

Skilled negotiators balance assertiveness with fairness and maintain professionalism throughout the Negotiation process.

4) Compromising Negotiation

Compromising Negotiation involves finding a middle ground where both parties make concessions to reach a satisfactory agreement.

It is a give-and-take approach that focuses on finding an acceptable solution rather than maximizing individual gains.

Compromising Negotiation can be useful when time is limited or when both parties are equally powerful.

It is also useful when both parties have similar levels of importance assigned to their outcomes.

Pamela B. Palafoxl

Skilled negotiators in Compromising Negotiation have the ability to identify and prioritize issues, evaluate trade-offs, and find mutually agreeable solutions.

5) Power-based Negotiation

Power-based Negotiation relies on the use of power, influence, and advantage to shape the Negotiation process and outcomes.

Negotiators with more power may exploit their advantage to assert their interests and gain favorable terms.

Power can come from various sources, such as position, expertise, or access to resources.

However, relying solely on Power-based Negotiation can strain relationships and lead to suboptimal outcomes.

Skilled negotiators understand the dynamics of power and use it judiciously.

They combine it with effective communication and relationship-building strategies

How to choose your Negotiation Type?
Understanding the different Types of Negotiation styles and selecting the most

a suitable one can significantly impact the process and results.

Here are some steps to help a person choose their Negotiation Type:

a) **Self-awareness:** Understand your personality, communication style, and preferences. Consider whether you tend to be assertive or accommodating, competitive or cooperative.

Reflect on your strengths and weaknesses in Negotiations and any cultural or societal influences that might impact your approach.

b) **Identify the situation**: Each Negotiation scenario is unique with different context. So, determine the nature of the Negotiation - is it a win-win scenario, where both parties can benefit, or a win-lose situation where one party gains at the expense of the other?

Also, assess the level of trust and the existing relationship between the parties involved.

c) **Research** **and** **preparation**: Gather information about the other party, their interests, goals, and possible Negotiation styles.

Also, understand the subject matter and the various options available.

Adequate preparation will boost your confidence and flexibility during the Negotiation process.

d) Consider collaborative Negotiation: In most cases, a Collaborative or Integrative Negotiation style is recommended.

This approach focuses on finding mutually beneficial solutions.

This helps foster long-term relationships and maintains open communication.

It is particularly useful when the parties have common goals and interests.

e) Competitive Negotiation when necessary: A Competitive or Distributive Negotiation style may be appropriate in some situations.

It is necessary when resources are limited, or interests are directly opposed.

However, this style can be risky, as it may harm relationships and lead to suboptimal outcomes.

f) Be flexible: A successful negotiator must be adaptable and know when to switch between different Negotiation styles.

Therefore, being able to transition from a competitive to a collaborative approach or vice versa can be a valuable skill.

Pamela B. Palafoxl

g) Active listening and empathy: Regardless Negotiation style chosen, active listening and empathy are essential.

Understanding the other party's perspectives and needs will aid in building rapport and finding common ground.

h) Seek win-win solutions: Strive for win-win outcomes whenever possible, where both parties feel satisfied with the agreement.

Such agreements are more likely to be sustainable and lead to future cooperation.

(j) Evaluate and learn: After the Negotiation, assess the results and your chosen Negotiation style.

Identify areas for improvement and learn from the experience to enhance your future Negotiation skills.

Learn about a structured approach to Sales and Negotiate great deals by signing up for our Sales Bootcamp Course now!

Tips for effective Negotiation

Pamela B. Palafoxl

Here are some tips that you can use in your next Negotiation:

•Use numbers instead of ranges
When it comes to financial Negotiations,

•opting for precise numerical values over vague ranges is a strategic move that yields multiple advantages.

Firstly, by refraining from presenting a range, you effectively shield your minimum acceptable amount from the other party.

This can be a pivotal aspect of Negotiation, as divulging your lower limit may weaken your position and potentially lead to less favorable outcomes.

Additionally, this approach carries a significant benefit.

It's the demonstration of thorough research and preparation.

When you present a concrete figure like GBP 4,560 instead of rounding it to GBP 4,000, it communicates to the other party that you've meticulously assessed the pricing landscape.

This signals your commitment to achieving a fair and well-considered deal, making you appear more credible and informed.

As a result, this can bolster your position in the Negotiation and instill confidence in the other party that they are dealing with a knowledgeable and well-prepared counterpart.

The use of precise numbers is a strategic tool that not only safeguards your minimum threshold but also bolsters your Negotiation credibility.

This also helps position you favorably in the eyes of the other party.

•Ask open-ended questions

Utilizing open-ended questions is a valuable technique to gain insights into the other party's circumstances, thereby providing you with leverage for the ongoing discussions.

To illustrate this with an example, let's consider a scenario where you represent an apartment leasing company engaged in Negotiations with a vendor providing painting services.

In this context, employing open-ended questions proves highly effective.

Instead of asking a closed, specific question like, "Are painting and wall repair services included?" which could lead to a straightforward 'yes' or 'no' response, you can employ a more open-ended approach.

For instance, you may inquire, "What services are you willing to offer for this price?" This open-ended question encourages the vendor to provide a comprehensive breakdown of the services they are prepared to include within the contract.

The use of open-ended questions acts as a catalyst for detailed responses, facilitating a deeper understanding of the vendor's offerings.

Furthermore, this approach can uncover additional services and provisions that the vendor might be willing to include, which might not have surfaced in response to a closed-ended query.

Ultimately, these open-ended questions enhance your Negotiation tactics by equipping you with valuable information that can be harnessed as leverage during the bargaining process.

•Consider your timing

The element of timing carries substantial weight in Negotiations as it can significantly impact the outcome.

In numerous industries, there exists an optimal window for procuring services, which frequently occurs at the conclusion of a month or quarter.

This particular time frame aligns with the period when sales personnel and vendors must meet their assigned quotas.

As a result, they may be more inclined to make concessions or provide favorable terms to close deals within this time frame.

More importantly, the significance of timing should not be overlooked during the Negotiation process itself.

The specific moment when you choose to make a request or a concession can be as crucial as the content of the request or concession.

Consider this scenario: waiting until you find yourself in a stronger position within the Negotiation that provides you with enhanced bargaining power when making demands.

This strategic delay, aligned with a favorable position, can effectively tip the scales in your favor, increasing the likelihood of achieving more favorable terms or outcomes.

CHAPTER 4

The Principled Negotiation?

Today, negotiation is one of the most sought-after mechanisms for settling differences without fighting.

In principled negotiation, compromises and agreements are reached while avoiding disputes and arguments.

Principled negotiation, also known as integrative negotiation, employs a method that integrates the interests of each party to find a compromise.

Pamela B. Palafoxl

It allows one to move past the position of a win/lose mentality and focus on the negotiation.

The approach is popularly known as the "win-win" method since it focuses on the interests of the parties involved and removes the "all-or-nothing" attitude.

What is principled Negotiation?

Many people view negotiations as a blood sport, winner-take-all scenario.

The winner gets the bigger piece of the pie; the loser slinks away feeling defeated and demoralized.

This "divide the pie" approach is called distributive bargaining. Both sides stake out a position and go to battle.

Pamela B. Palafoxl

Whereas distributive bargaining is position-based, principled negotiation is interest-based.

Interests can include concerns, desires, fears, and needs that are important to a side.

Principled negotiation also operates under the assumption that the two parties are interested in maintaining a business relationship after the deal is done.

Principled negotiation is also known as win-win negotiation or integrative negotiation.

The term "integrative" is used because the two parties' interests are considered in

combination, so there's the possibility of creating joint value - a win-win scenario.

Pamela B. Palafoxl

The key is a spirit of collaboration and cooperation, not competition.

Advantages of Principled Negotiation
Enables parties to resolve conflicting issues peacefully, without fighting over competing demands.

This helps maintain positive future interaction between the parties involved.

An efficient way of settling disputes, since all interests are explored during negotiation, and each party is given mutual consideration.

Results in a concrete decision where all parties feel their interests are considered, and no one is a winner or loser, but they have created a win-win scenario.

Limitations of Principled Negotiation

Pamela B. Palafoxl

Limitations of principled negotiation include;
•There is the possibility of biased dispute-resolution, especially when one party is dishonest.

•Basing the negotiation on interest and not position may make agreement impossible, especially when the issue at hand and the personal interests conflict.

The approach is vulnerable to negotiation errors.

•lack of cooperation and miscommunication, especially due to varying interests.

The approach is sometimes considered to oversimplify things, since it lays numerous guidelines and approaches on negotiations.

Applying multiple rules and guidelines, in an attempt to mainstream the negotiation, limits the ability of the negotiating parties to fully express their interests.

Lesson

Tenets of Principled Negotiation
There are four main tenets to principled negotiation:

•Separate the people from the problem - Emotions and people problems, like faulty perceptions or poor communication, can

cloud a negotiation and detract from the substantive issues.

•Focus on interests, not positions - Negotiations should be about getting what you really need, not staking out an arbitrary position and defending it at all costs.

Pamela B. Palafoxl

•Expand the pie - Look for a way to provide mutual gain; maybe expand the discussion to include other elements so that both parties can feel they came out of the negotiation with a win.

•Insist on objective criteria - Look for outside guidance on what's fair.

For example, if you're buying a house, your agent can do a comparative market analysis to see what similar houses have been selling for in the neighborhood.

Pamela B. Palafoxl

CHAPTER 5

Negotiation Tips

T o successfully separate the people from the problem, consider the following tips.

1 Treat every relationship as a long term relationship.

You never know when someone you are negotiating with might make subsequent appearances in your work life, or become your next door neighbor.

The point here is that no one can fully predict the future, nor can they predict when and how you might need to work with someone in the future.

Pamela B. Palafoxl

So, to make life easier on yourself and others, imagine that every relationship you encounter is a long term relationship.

This is guaranteed to help your negotiations – and your life – run smoother;

2•Model respectful behavior, regardless of how you are being treated. If the other negotiator articulates an insulting slur, do not do the same.

Rather, turn the other cheek and continue on with the negotiation, or address the comment in a manner that is respectful and that prioritizes both the negotiators' relationship and the negotiation process.

If you model this respectful behavior and clearly establish that the objective of this negotiation is to address the problem, your fellow negotiator will likely also come to see that

•(1) his/her personal slurs are ineffective and/or

Pamela B. Palafoxl

•(2) he/she is thwarting the development of a solution for both of you;

3•Try to frame yourself, and see the other, as an ally with whom you are working with against a mutual problem.

If you see your fellow negotiator as an ally, you mentally place yourself on the same team as him/her.

This minimizes the tendency for you and the other negotiator to villainize each other.

Framing yourself as an ally also encourages collaboration, making you more accommodating to your counterpart and, in return, your counterpart more accommodating to you;

4•Try to remember 'Be hard on the issues, not on the people.'

Use this insightful tip to replace any negative mantra running through your head.

Pamela B. Palafoxl

This tip embodies the idea of separating the people from the problem.

Focus on the issues and make sure that they are fully addressed, but go easy on the people.

They are the ones you must work with to best address the issues, and they may be
people you will need to work with well into the future;

5•If appropriate, set ground rules that vocally prioritize the relationship.

This can be a very helpful tool! If both negotiators agree at the onset to prioritize

their relationship, then this ground rule can be referenced in any future instance where one negotiator feels like the negotiation is turning into a personal attack.

Furthermore, since both negotiators must agree to this ground rule at the onset, it primes the negotiation to be a successful process that focuses on the issues and not on the people;

Pamela B. Palafoxl

6•Avoid trading the relationship for the substance.

If you find yourself in a position where the other negotiator is covertly asking you to trade something of substance in order to maintain a good relationship with him/her or his/her organization, stop.

Think hard before you decide to give up one of your interests in order to maintain a good relationship with your counterpart.

While this may result in a better long-term relationship, it may just as likely result in a relationship where the other believes that you can be easily taken for a ride.

7•Likewise, you should also avoid making a proposition that trades relationships for substance.

While you may receive a concession this way, the implementation of the deal and the relationship between negotiators will suffer.

Pamela B. Palafoxl

When interests and emotions are high, it is easy to turn a negotiation into a boxing ring where you want nothing more than to defeat

the other person – and possibly bruise their reputation and self-esteem in the process.

Avoid this. In the end, such actions will only lead to a lousy negotiation deal and a tarnished relationship between negotiators.

8•Instead, prioritize the relationship shared between negotiators, separate the people from the problem, and act in a manner that clearly communicates your priorities to your fellow negotiator.

This will ensure a smoother negotiation process – from conception to implementation – and will help maintain a strong working relationship between negotiators.

Pamela B. Palafoxl

CHAPTER 6

Real Estate Team Lead

n estate team,when most people think of real estate agents, they think of a professional who works solo.
And sometimes, that's actually the case.

Anyone can obtain a real estate license and start taking clients, and they often become quite successful.

Drive through any neighborhood, and you'll probably see a "for sale" sign with a realtor's name and photograph prominently displayed.

Pamela B. Palafoxl

That said, many real estate agents instead choose to work as part of a team.

Teams can support each-other and share their workloads, and each team member has unique skills to bring to the table.

Joining a team can be a great way to grow your business, but there are also some drawbacks to be aware of.

Here's everything you need to know about real estate teams, how they work, and how to build one.

How Are Real Estate Teams Structured?
A real estate team is a group of two or more real estate agents who pool their resources.

Team members split their commissions and can even help out with each other's clients.

For example, suppose you're overbooked on Monday, and your teammate Jenny is overbooked on Wednesday.

Jenny could handle some of your showings on Monday, and you could return the favor on Wednesday.

Because you're splitting commissions, everybody has good reason to support the whole team.

Different real estate teams have different structures, and there's no single "right" way of doing things.

With larger teams, different agents sometimes work on specific tasks.

For example, one could be in charge of dealing with lenders, another could be responsible for open houses, another might handle phone calls, etc.

This allows team members to work in roles that play to their strengths, making the entire team more effective.

Real Estate Team Lead

In most, but not all cases, a real estate team will have a team leader.

Pamela B. Palafoxl

This is normally the agent who takes care of the listings, while other team members will meet with potential buyers.

In some teams, all team members create listings, but the team lead still brings in most of the business.

In some cases, an agent from within the team might be representing the buyer.

This creates a situation known as dual-agency.

In dual-agency, the team leader represents the seller, while the team member represents the buyer.

This can be managed without creating a conflict of interest, but if you're a buyer, it's

wise to ask your agent about any potential conflicts, and how they avoid them.

Real Estate Team Models
There are many ways to structure a real estate team.

The optimal structure will depend on the agents' levels of experience, how many agents there are, and each agent's strengths and weaknesses.

That said, most teams use one of the following three models:

Mentor/Mentee Real Estate Team
The mentor/mentee team structure is exactly what it sounds like.

The team leader is an experienced agent, while the other agents are new and inexperienced.

For the newer agents, the benefits are obvious. Instead of having to go it alone,

you get the benefit of a mentor with years or decades of experience in the field.

For the team lead, the hope is that their mentoring will pay off in the long run.

Pamela B. Palafoxl

As the newer agents learn and grow, they'll contribute more and more to the team's bottom line.

Team Leader Model
The team leader model works best when one agent has a very strong personal brand.

If an agent's name and face is well-known in the community, there might not be enough hours in the day to keep up with the demand.

An agent with this kind of presence can build a team around them to help lighten the load.

There are typically strict branding guidelines for other team members in this arrangement.

For example, an experienced agent named John Smith might call his team "John Smith Realtors" and require other team members to put that on their letterheads.

Lead Team Model

The lead team model is the opposite of the team leader model.

Instead of one team member making all the decisions and dictating the branding, several real estate agents come together and work as equals.

This most often happens when agents have different skill sets that work well together.

For example, one agent might be a whiz at conducting open houses, but struggle with phone communication.

They could partner with another agent with strong phone skills, and so on.

At the end of the day, everyone gets to focus on what they're most comfortable with, and the team is stronger for it.

Pros & Cons Of Real Estate Teams
There are costs and benefits to working with a real estate team – for the agents themselves and buyers and sellers.

Let's talk about some of the pros and cons.

Pros Of Joining A Real Estate Team
A larger resource pool – When you work as a solo real estate agent, you have to do

everything yourself, from marketing to open houses to closings.

A group of agents gives you access to more leads and the resources to invest in high-quality marketing material.

A supportive environment – Working as an individual environment can be lonely.

If you fall into a funk, there's nobody around to give you advice, help you out, or hold you accountable.

This can turn into a vicious cycle that damages your career. With a team, you'll have people around you to provide that support.

Pamela B. Palafoxl

You'll also be able to improve your own skills by helping others.

Leads, leads, and more leads – Leads are the life's blood of the real estate business.

Without leads, you don't have any clients.

The more agents are looking for leads, the more you'll have to work with.

Oftentimes, different agents have better insight into different areas, so your leads will also have more geographic diversity.

Professional development – If you just got your real estate license, there's probably a lot you don't know.

•How do you find leads and convert them into clients?

•How do you create listings to attract potential buyers?

Pamela B. Palafoxl

By joining a team with an experienced lead, you'll get all the advice and guidance you need to grow your career.

Even if you want to work as an individual agent, it's not a bad idea to work for a team for a few years to learn and grow.

Benefits for clients – As a client, a real estate team gives you access to a deeper pool of knowledge and experience than any individual agent.

And if your agent is unavailable for some reason, another team member will be able to help you out.

This all comes with the same commission cost as hiring a single agent.

Cons Of Joining A Real Estate Team.

A toxic work environment – Ideally, you'll be working with a group of people who mesh well together and create a supportive environment.

But sometimes, people just don't get along, which creates a toxic environment.

Pamela B. Palafoxl

Less control over your business – Even if your team uses the lead team model, you won't have full control over your business.

Decisions can only be made by consensus, which means you can't move forward with every idea you like.

No personal branding – If you're trying to build your personal brand, working for a team is nowhere nearly as effective as working under your own name.

All the marketing will put the team name front and center.

Drawbacks for clients – Depending on how the team operates, you might be working with a different agent at each point in the sales process.

This might not bother you, but many people prefer to work with the same person throughout the entire process.

Who Should Join A Real Estate Team?

Pamela B. Palafoxl

•Joining a real estate team is generally a good idea for newly-licensed agents who need to grow and develop.

•However, it's also a good idea if you're a true master of one aspect of the real estate process.

You can partner with other people who specialize in other aspects, and create a top-tier team.

•If you've recently relocated and don't have a strong local network, it's also well worth considering.

If you've already got a strong network and are doing plenty of business, joining a team makes less sense.

When To Start A Real Estate Team

Starting a real estate team is a different ball game altogether.

Take a look at your schedule; if there's a ton of free time for finding customers, you're probably not ready to start a team.

•The average real estate agent has enough time to handle around 50 to 60 transactions per year.

•When your brand is strong enough that you're turning away customers,your only way to grow your income is to start a team.

Of course, leading a team has its own complications.

The accounting is more complex, and **you have to** set aside some of your own time for coaching, mentoring, and recruiting new team members.

If none of that appeals to you, you might prefer to work solo for the rest of your career.

How to build a real estate team

•When most people think of real estate agents, they think of a professional who works solo.

Pamela B. Palafoxl

And sometimes, that's actually the case.

•Anyone can obtain a real estate license and start taking clients, and they often become quite successful.

•Drive through any neighborhood, and you'll probably see a "for sale" sign with a realtor's name and photograph prominently displayed.

That said, many real estate agents instead choose to work as part of a team.

Teams can support each-other and share their workloads, and each team member has unique skills to bring to the table.

Joining a team is part of the great way to grow your business

Pamela B. Palafoxl

CONCLUSION

et out on a groundbreaking journey in "Bargaining with Result," where the power of discussion meets the craft of achieving phenomenal results.

This book rethinks the way we see haggling through enthralling stories, viable methodologies, and provocative experiences, advising us that the genuine substance of exchange lies in getting what we need as well as making significant, lasting outcomes.

Whether you're a seasoned negotiator or just starting out,"Bargaining with Result" will teach you how to discover hidden potential, seize

Pamela B. Palafoxl

opportunities, and master the art of achieving extraordinary success.

Prepare to rethink your strategy, rewrite your story, and embrace a future in which every negotiation serves as a stepping stone to greatness.

Are you ready to push the boundaries of what's possible? Your journey begins right now.

Pamela B. Palafoxl

www.ingramcontent.com/pod-product-compliance
Lightning Source LLC
Chambersburg PA
CBHW071211290526
45796CB00008B/210